PHOTOGRAPHER'S GUIDE TO
WASHINGTON'S BEST VIEWS

PHOTOGRAPHER'S GUIDE TO
WASHINGTON'S BEST VIEWS

VOLUME I - MT. RAINIER

New Edition

ROLLIN GEPPERT

ARPress
ILLUMINATING IDEAS.
EMPOWERING VOICES

ARPress
45 Dan Road Suite 5
Canton MA 02021

Hotline: 1(888) 821-0229
Fax: 1(508) 545-7580

Ordering Information:
Quantity sales. Special discounts are available on quantity purchases by corporations, associations, and others. For details, contact the publisher at the address above.

Printed in the United States of America.

ISBN-13:	Softcover	979-8-89356-967-4
	eBook	979-8-89356-968-1

Library of Congress Control Number: 2024910099

FOREWORD

Photographer Rollin Geppert lives in Olympia, Washington and through eBooks, his website, www.Geppertphotography.com, fine art prints and other published works, shares his 50 years of experience in searching out some of the best views in Washington State from which to photograph the scenic beauty of nature.

Mount Rainier, the largest of the five major volcanic mountains in the state, is featured in this 2024 revised Volume I of his **Photographer's Guide to Washington's Best Views**.

Proceeds from the sale of the Photographer's Guide to Washington's Best Views will be donated to the Ecosystems Scholarship Fund (www.Ecoscholarfund.org) which provides financial aid to college students majoring in natural resources and land use planning.

PREFACE

There are five major volcanic mountains in Washington State and when teamed with their associated landscapes draw significant attention from photographers, tourists and residents alike. With foregrounds of forests, lakes, rivers, meadows, wildflowers and wildlife the combinations for great photographs are limitless. The viewpoints in this book are ones I discovered while exploring the main highways and back roads both by automobile and motorcycle. Think of using the **Photographer's Guide to Washington's Best Views** as a combination of a roadside guide and geocaching adventure, where the treasure is the photograph. What makes this book unique is that the locations are ones that you can drive to without any long-distance hiking. It's the locations that are the most important. There are many other books that address scenic views within the park, but this book is one of a very few that address scenic views outside of the park.

I hope this book of my favorite Mt. Rainier views provides you with an incentive to locate these visual treasures of nature, and then to go on exploring with the knowledge that more special places may be just around the next bend in the road.

My driving directions will get you to the "magic spot." However, return trips may be needed to get the type of image you want. All of these sites are accessible using an automobile such as the average sedan. Most of these sites are open to the public but if you have any doubt, please obtain permission from the landowner before setting up your tripod. Also, be sure to display the necessary permits and passes issued by the United States Forest Service, Washington State and National Park Service.

There are many locations from which you can see Mt. Rainier but my book provides you with enough information to find the 60 geographic locations I consider having prime views of Mt. Rainier. By entering the latitude and longitude of each site into a Geographic Positioning System (GPS) you will be able to drive to the site. If you are using a standard road map, the driving directions can be used to locate these sites. In some cases, a short walk is required. For the most part, however, these sites are readily accessible from major paved roads and a few gravel roads, all of which are suitable for the average vehicle. No 4-wheel drive vehicle is necessary. My goal is to make these sites appealing and readily accessible to everyone.

The photographs in this book were made using a combination of cameras and formats. In the beginning, 1971, I used a variety of Canon 35mm SLR cameras loaded with Kodachrome and later with Fujichrome color transparency films. As my passion for photography grew, I started including medium formats (120) using Mamiya, Pentax, Hasselblad and Bronica cameras. The best photographs were then scanned into TIFF files. Since 2007 I have used Canon digital SLR cameras and the following lenses: 17-40, 28-70, 24-105, 70-200, 300 and 400mm focal lengths.

Regarding the use of filters, I will occasionally use a polarizer or graduated filter. HDR (high dynamic range) techniques have been used sparingly. My goal has been to render the final photograph as close as possible to the conditions under which I saw it while making the original photograph.

Sometimes it is possible to achieve a great landscape photograph during lighting conditions that seem to last forever. More often than not, great lighting lasts a very short period of time and selecting the "decisive moment" becomes crucial. Sometimes it's a matter of a few seconds and other times it can be many minutes. Stormy weather with high winds aloft tend to move clouds quickly and the resulting lighting can change equally as fast.

I am not identifying a specific time of day to best capture a photograph from each site. You, the reader and photographer, can define what you believe to be the prime time for your photograph. These photographs were taken over a period of 50 + years, each having a unique lighting condition, all the way from before sunrise to after sunset. Some were taken during the mid-day when some professional photographers believe the lighting is far from perfect.

Through these photos I have worked to capture a wide variety of lighting conditions designed to evoke an equally wide range of emotions from the viewer. In some you will see a blue-bird sky with a nary cloud. In others you will see the mountain shrouded in clouds and in some cases actually making its own weather, most notably the "lenticular" cloud layer that looks like a hat or cap perched near or over the summit.

Creating a great photograph at these sites is up to you. Remember, repeat trips to these spots may be needed before you get that special photograph that brings you great satisfaction. Hopefully, you will find these views as beautiful in person as I have worked to illustrate in this book. My goal is for you to create photographs that bring you great joy. In some photos I have intentionally created a juxtaposition of the mountain and items of the man-made world.

However, in most of the photos I have selectively framed the scene in order to eliminate most if not all man-made components.

The Mt. Rainier photographs are arranged to show the views possible by traveling the highways bordering all sides of the mountain and from within the boundaries of the Mount Rainier National Park. My favorite sites are the ones viewing east, mostly late in the day from September through February when the mountain is covered with snow and the skies are deep blue or filled with stormy gray-blue clouds. People out for an afternoon or early evening drive traveling the north-south oriented roads stand the best chance of seeing these views as they look to the east.

Please keep in mind that the natural beauty you came to photograph should not be harmed during the photo making process. Especially within the boundaries of Mount Rainier National Park, follow the warning signs such as staying on the trails, not swimming in the lakes, not trampling or cutting the vegetation along the shorelines, controlling your pets and being very careful with the use of fire.

Using this book is easy. The explanations below provide the information you will need to start your photography treasure hunt. Enter the latitude and longitude coordinates into a GPS or follow the driving directions to locate each site. Specifically, here is how it works:

Latitude: Units of measurement are listed in degrees (up to six decimal places) north (N) of the equator.

Longitude: Units of measurement are listed in degrees (up to six decimal places) west (W) of the Prime Meridian in Greenwich, England.

Road #: The road number or name is the primary road on which the site is located. It could be an interstate highway (I-5), a Washington State Highway Route (Hwy), a United States Highway (US), a National Forest Development Road (FR), a city street or a city avenue.

Nearest Town: An incorporated town or city located close to the site.

Access: The actual driving directions in miles, directions to turn, road names and/or numbers and mile post (MP) numbers, where available. Additionally, this includes advisories on vehicle parking, landowner permission, and direction of view and sometimes data on the photographic equipment I used to make each photo.

Copyright 2011, revised in 2024, by Rollin Geppert

For information regarding the use of these and other photos for publication, advertising or fine art prints, please contact Rollin Geppert at www.Geppertphotography.com or Rgeppert@comcast.net.

On The Front Cover: When the sun rises behind Mt. Rainier, the shadow of the mountain is sometimes projected on the high clouds above. Here you can see the shadows on all three summits. I have never seen this in any publication. This phenomenon is very rare and when it occurs it can be observed from many locations from Tacoma to Centralia.

This map may be helpful to you when using my driving directions. The photographs are arranged in five chapters for the views visible from the west (my favorite), east, north, south and from within the Mount Rainier National Park.

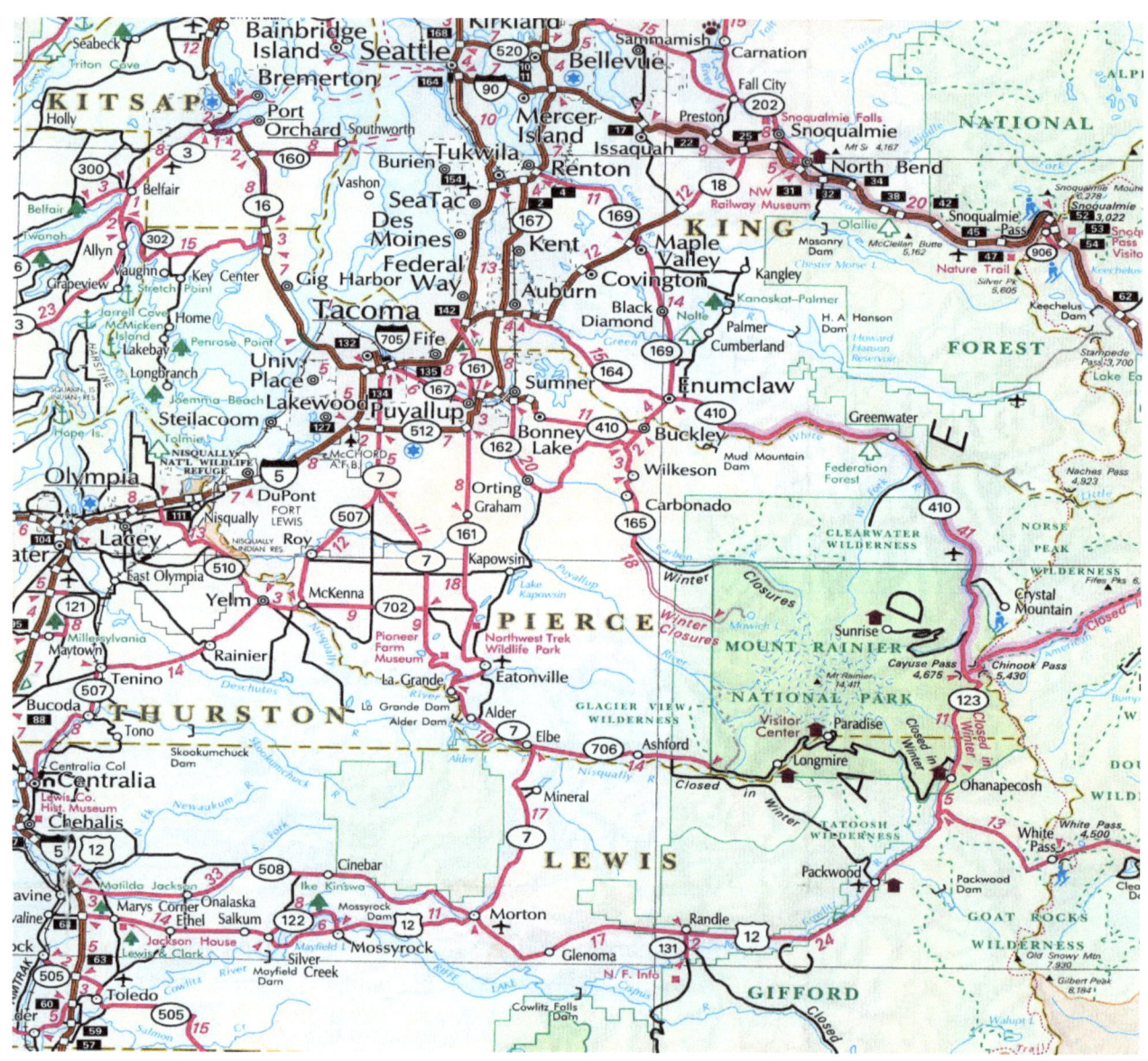

MOUNT RAINIER

Mount Rainier is a massive stratovolcano located 54 miles southeast of Seattle in the state of Washington, United States with a summit elevation of 14,410 feet. It is the highest mountain in Washington and the Cascade Range. It has a topographic prominence of 13,211 feet, greater than that of K2 (13,189 feet). On clear days it dominates the southeastern horizon in most of the Seattle-Tacoma metropolitan area to such an extent that locals often refer to it simply as "The Mountain." On days of exceptional clarity, it can also be seen from as far away as Portland, Oregon, and Victoria, British Columbia. The British explorer, Captain George Vancouver, discovered the mountain in 1792 and named it for a fellow naval officer, Peter Regneir, now spelled Rainier.

The Carbon, Puyallup, Mowich, Nisqually, and Cowlitz Rivers begin as eponymous glaciers of Mount Rainier. The sources of the White River are Winthrop, Emmons, and Fryingpan Glaciers. The White, Carbon, and Mowich join the Puyallup River, which discharges into Commencement Bay at Tacoma; the Nisqually empties into Puget Sound east of Lacey; and the Cowlitz joins the Columbia River between Kelso and Longview.

Moisture laden weather systems move inland from the Pacific Ocean, battering Mount Rainier, and drop record-setting quantities of snow at the higher elevations before drifting eastward. The total precipitation, approximately 87 inches annually at Longmire and 126 inches at Paradise, shapes the 26 major glaciers and 36 square miles of permanent snowfields and glaciers making Mount Rainier the most heavily glaciated peak in the lower 48 states.

Mt. Rainier is the tallest of the fifteen great volcanoes, from Mount Garibaldi in British Columbia to Lassen Peak in California, that make up the backbone of the Cascade Range. These peaks, part of the 1,000-volcano Ring of Fire that surrounds the Pacific Ocean, are known to geologists as stratovolcanoes -- steep sided cones composed of thousands of layers of lava and ash erupted during their million-year lifespan. Mt. Rainier is considered one of the most dangerous volcanoes in the world, and it is on the Decade Volcano list. Because of its large amount of glacial ice, Mt. Rainier could potentially produce massive lahars that would threaten the whole Puyallup River valley.

Mount Rainier National Park is managed by the United States National Park Service which is part of the United States Department of Interior. The park is located in southeast Pierce County and northeast Lewis County. It's one of our nation's oldest National Parks, having been established on March 2, 1899 as the fifth national park in the United States. The park contains 368 square miles (235,520 acres) including all of Mt. Rainier. In 2023 1.67 million people visited the park. Consult the park's web site prior to visiting the park in order to get the latest road, trail and weather information.

CONTENTS

CHAPTER 1
VIEWING EAST

In my opinion the best views are looking east to Mt. Rainier whether it's at sunrise, mid-day or sunset.

In this chapter the sites are arranged traveling from north to south starting in Seattle with an iconic view from Kerry Park on Queen Anne Hill and progressing south with views from Tacoma, Gig Harbor, Olympia, Rainier, Eatonville, Ashford, Elbe and Mineral.

Seattle (Kerry Park)

Latitude: N47.62958
Longitude: W122.35978
Road #: West Highland Drive on Queen Anne Hill
Nearest Town: Seattle, WA
Access: From downtown Seattle, take Denny Way west to Queen Anne Avenue North, go north up one of the steepest hills in town, turn left (west) on West Highland Drive for 2.5 blocks. Kerry Park is on the left and provides one of the best views of Seattle Space Needle, Elliott Bay and Mount Rainier. This site is 61 airline miles from the summit. A late day photo is best when taken within 45 minutes of sunset. At ISO 100, a good place to start with your exposure is f/8 at 15 seconds.

Longbranch

Latitude: N47.210162
Longitude: W122.757352
Road #: Key Peninsula Highway South
Nearest Town: Purdy, WA

Access: From downtown Purdy, just west of #16, take #302 southwest for 18 miles to Longbranch, an unincorporated community in Pierce County, located on the Key Peninsula, along Filucy Bay between Pitt Passage and Balch Passage.

Longbranch is primarily residential and includes a marina, church, and community center known as the Longbranch Improvement which was founded in 1921.

SeaTac

Latitude: N47.43518
Longitude: W122.27122
Road #: Military Road SE
Nearest SeaTac, WA
Access: From the south or the north, take Exit 152 off I-5 and go west back under I-5 on S 188th Street and turn right (north) on Military Road S, 0.1 mile, at the north end is vantage point. This site is approximately 1/2 block south of the intersection with 186th Street and Military Road S near house numbers 19515-19605. From the airport take the Pacific Highway S (also known as Old #99 or International Way) and go east on S 188th Street to Military Road S and 186th Street.

Ruston/Tacoma

Latitude: N47.29931
Longitude: W122.51028
Road #: Ruston Way
Nearest Town: Tacoma, WA
Access: From downtown Tacoma go north on #705, continue on Schuster Parkway which turns into Ruston Way. Almost anywhere along Ruston Way is good for viewing Mt. Rainier especially from some of restaurant's parking lots. A stellar view is available from the Commencement Condos on North Bennett Street but you will need permission to enter the building.

Tacoma Narrows Bridge

Latitude: N47.275694
Longitude: W122.560434
Road: Hwy #16
Nearest Town: Tacoma:
Access: From the intersection of I-5 and Highway #16, go west on #16, crossing the bridge over the Tacoma Narrows and exit on 24th Street NW, crossing west over #16, turn left (south) on Jahn Ave. NW, go to end of road and turn left (east) on Stone Drive NW and continue south just before it meets Weatherswood Drive NW. This is the spot.

Tacoma Narrows Park

Latitude: N47.267484
Longitude: W122.564450
Road: Doc's Drive
Nearest Town: Tacoma:
Access: From the intersection exit on 24th Street of I-5 and Highway #16, go west on #16, crossing the bridge over the Tacoma Narrows and exit on 24th Street NW, crossing west over #16, turn left (south) on Jahn Ave. NW, go to end of road (a "T") and turn left (east) on Stone Drive NW and continue south on Lucille Parkway NW and continue on Doc's Drive to the Tacoma Narrows Park.

Gig Harbor

Latitude: N47.339041
Longitude: W122.591880
Road #: Franklin St.
Nearest Town: Gig Harbor, WA
Access: From downtown Gig Harbor, take Harborview Drive along the south side of the harbor for 0.9 miles, turn right (northeast) and continue on Harborview Drive for ½ block, turn left on Burnham Drive, go one block and turn right on Franklin Street and look to the east between the closely spaced houses in the 8800 to 8900 block for this view. This view is probably the iconic view for all of Gig Harbor. A 250-280mm lens is appropriate.

Sunrise Beach

Latitude: N47.35778
Longitude: W122.56066
Road #: Moller Drive NW
Nearest Town: Gig Harbor, WA
Access: From downtown Gig Harbor, take Harborview Drive along the south side of the harbor for 0.9 mile, turn right (northeast) and continue on Harborview Drive for 0.7 mile, turn right on 96th St. NW and go 0.3 mile, turn right on Crescent Valley Drive NW and go 0.3 mile, turn left on Dana Drive NW and go up hill for 1.9 miles, small dip in the road among these residential homes, view east overlooking Sunrise Beach to Commencement Bay and Tacoma. The small dot on the water is the ferry that runs from Point Defiance to Vashon Island.

Fox Island

Latitude: N47.274091
Longitude: W122.651071
Road #: Fox Island Bridge Road NW
Nearest Town: Gig Harbor

Access: From #16 at the Gig Habor exit, go southwest on Wollochet Dr. SW, right (west) on 40th St. W, left (south) on 70th Ave. NW and continue south/southwest on Warren Dr. NW, south across the Fox Island Bridge Road NW. At the south end of the bridge park at the Fox Island Boat Ramp. Cross over to the pedestrian sidewalk, where it's safe to set your tripod, and your view will be to the southeast.

Fort Lewis

Latitude: N47.13351
Longitude: W122.61308
Road #: DuPont-Steilacoom Road
Nearest Town: DuPont, WA
Access: From I-5 exit #119 to Old DuPont, drive north on DuPont-Steilacoom Road heading to Steilacoom for 3.1 miles, stopping just south of East Drive. The view is east from the shoulder of the DuPont-Steilacoom Road. This is the old Fort Lewis US Army base (now called Joint Base Lewis-McCord) and may have special restrictions on photography. The buildings in this photo are troop barracks some dating back to 1920's. It's another 2.7 miles to downtown Steilacoom, incorporated in 1854, the first incorporated town in what is now Washington State.

Puget Marina

Latitude: N47.14899
Longitude: W122.79384
Road #: Johnson Point Road
Nearest Town: Olympia, WA
Access: From downtown Olympia, take South Bay Road north which turns into Johnson Point Road; turn right (east) on 78th Ave. NE for 0.9 mile, then left on Walnut Road NE for 0.4 mile. Park at the Puget Marina and ask for permission to walk down the road accessing the boat launch. The view is to the east overlooking the Nisqually Reach. This photo was made one hour before sunrise in October.

Nisqually Reach

Latitude: N47.16637
Longitude: W122.81241
Road #: Johnson Point Road
Nearest Town: Olympia, WA
Access: From downtown Olympia take South Bay Road north which turns into Johnson Point Road, turn right (east) on 92nd Ave. towards Zittel's Marina. Lohrer St. is on the left and there are a number of homes having this view. Landowner permission is required to gain access to the waterfront. This photo was made using a 300mm lens and a double exposure at dusk the day before full moon.

Luhr Beach

Latitude: N47.10104
Longitude: W122.72789
Road #: D'Milluhr Road NE
Nearest Town: Lacey, WA
Access: From Marvin Road/Martin Way SE intersection, go east on Martin Way 1.1 miles, turn left on Meridian Road NE for 0.4 mile crossing over I-5 to the roundabout, north on Meridian Road NE, turn right on 46th Ave. NE and go 0.2 mile, turn left on D'Milluhr Road NE and follow the signs to the public boat launch. at Luhr Beach and the Nisqually Reach Nature Center, a great place to get acquainted with the natural history of South Puget Sound's estuaries. A parking pass is required.

Steamboat Island

Latitude: N47.18193
Longitude: W122.94036
Road #: Steamboat Island Road Northwest
Nearest Town: Olympia, WA
Access: Heading west from Olympia on Hwy. #101, mile post 359.6, turn north on Steamboat Island Road NW for 9.1 miles to the bridge connecting the mainland with Steamboat Island. From the south end of the bridge the view is east across the marina to Mt. Rainier.

Kite Park

Latitude: N47.128940
Longitude: W122.176068
Road #: 198th Ave. E.
Nearest Town: Bonney Lake to the north and Orting to the south, WA
Access: From State Highway #410 in Bonney Lake, go southeast on South Prairie Rd. E for 0.2 mile and turn south on 198th Ave. E for 5 miles. Upslope from Kite Park is the Caffe' D'arte - Tehaleh Café which closes at 5pm. This photo was made using a 300mm focal length lens mounted on tripod located by the fire pit on the café patio.

Olympia, 4th Ave. Roundabout

Latitude: N47.04428
Longitude: W122.91238
Road #: 4th Ave W & Harrison Ave NW roundabout
Nearest Town: Olympia, WA
Access: From downtown Olympia, take 4th Ave West across the bridge over the southernmost tip of Budd Inlet to the northwest corner of the roundabout. Set up your tripod on the sidewalk. Parking is available on the side streets. This photo was made in early December using a 78mm focal length lens set at f/16 for 6 seconds, ISO 100.

Olympia, West Bay Drive

Latitude: N47.047636
Longitude: W122.912854
Road #: West Bay Drive NW
Nearest Town: Olympia, WA
Access: From downtown Olympia take 4th Ave. west across the bridge over the southernmost tip
of Budd Inlet and proceed through two traffic circles and turn right (north) on West Bay Drive
and go to #304 West Bay Drive and park on the street level parking lot located on the top floor of
the office/condo building. The view is east across the Olympia Yacht Club and Budd Inlet to the
downtown area and Mt. Rainier. Photo was made in November using a 400mm lens.

Olympia Country & Golf Course

Latitude: N47.08519
Longitude: W122.93600
Road #: Cooper Point Road
Nearest Town: Olympia, WA
Access: From downtown Olympia take the Cooper Point Road north, turn right on Country Club Road NW for 0.4 mile to the parking lot for the club. Take the paved path uphill past the Pro Shop to men's 10th Tee. The view is to the east across Budd Inlet. This photo was made using a 400mm lens.

Rainier the Town

Latitude: N46.88844
Longitude: W122.69767
Road #: Minnesota St. N. (turns into Rainier Road SE)
Nearest Town: Rainier, WA
Access: From downtown Rainier, take Minnesota St. N. northwest for 0.4 mile, under the railroad bridge, around the curve to the left and up the hill past the water tower. Parking is available at the top of the hill. This book would be incomplete without a photo of the mountain and the town with its name. You can see the mountain's ability to form its own weather with the infamous lenticular clouds that are sometimes referred to as flying saucers.

Lake Lawrence, Sunrise

Latitude: N46.850026
Longitude: W122.582389
Road #: Pleasant Beach Drive
Nearest Town: Yelm, WA
Access: From Yelm take Bald Hills Road SE to Four Corners, turn right on Vail Road SE, then left on Linday Road SE and right on Pleasant Beach Drive SE. For decades this site remained undeveloped but in 2018 or so a house was built on this site, thus permission from the owner is required. The 340-acre lake is stocked every spring with rainbow trout and channel catfish. Numerous bald eagles can be seen teaching their young how to fish. It's open to angling year-round. The lake has a boat launch maintained by the WA State Department of Fish and Wildlife.

Lake Lawrence, Sunset

Latitude: N46.850026
Longitude: W122.582389
Road #: Pleasant Beach Drive
Nearest Town: Yelm, WA
Access: From Yelm take Bald Hills Road SE to Four Corners, turn right on Vail Road SE, then left on Linday Road SE and right on Pleasant Beach Drive SE. For decades this site remained undeveloped but in 2018 or so a house was built on this site, thus permission from the owner is required. The 340-acre lake is stocked every spring with rainbow trout and channel catfish. Numerous bald eagles can be seen teaching their young how to fish. It's open to angling year-round. The lake has a boat launch maintained by the WA State Department of Fish and Wildlife.

Clear Lake

Latitude: N46.93057
Longitude: W122.28163
Road #: Hwy #161
Nearest Town: Eatonville, WA
Access: On #161, just 0.3 mile north of the Northwest Trek Wildlife Park, there is an opening that looks east across Clear Lake and the houses dotting the perimeter on the far shore. Parking is available on West Clear Lake Road, paralleling the west shoreline. Clear Lake is 155 acres in size with a maximum depth of 88 feet. This photo was made using 120mm focal length lens.

Dogwood Park

Latitude: N46.88443
Longitude: W122.30037
Road #: WA Highway #161
Nearest Town: Eatonville, WA
Access: From Eatonville, go northwest on Hwy #161 to within 0.2 mile of the intersection with the Eatonville Cutoff Road at Barney's Corner. There are two signs explaining this beautiful viewpoint, one of which is in this photo. The site was officially dedicated in a WA State Centennial ceremony on November 6, 1989. The two garden benches were purchased by the Dogwood Garden Club. The Blue Star Memorial Highway marker is a tribute to the Armed Forces that have defended the USA and was dedicated on September 14, 1994.

Eatonville Cutoff

Latitude: N46.820130
Longitude: W122.265499
Road #: Eatonville Cutoff Road
Nearest Town: Eatonville, WA
Access: From Eatonville, go south on the Eatonville Cutoff Road to mile post 1.5 and where the road makes a bend there is a small opening in the forest exposing this field. This site is near New Reliance which is a historic area but not signed as such on the highway but may be found on some maps. Another way to access this site is by starting at the intersection of Hwy. #7 and going north for 1.5 miles on the Eatonville Cutoff Road.

Eatonville

Latitude: N46.86456
Longitude: W122.26921
Road #: Orchard Ave. S.
Nearest Town: Eatonville, WA
Access: From city center, take the Eatonville Highway west out of town and just after the intersection with Center Street, turn southwest on Larson St. SW and continue as it changes into Orchard Ave. S heading south. Stop just short of the south end of Orchard Street to access many undeveloped housing lots facing east to the mountain. Landowner permission may be required. This is also a good place to include the town in the photo, especially if using a vertical format.

Tanwax Chapel

Latitude: N46.92555
Longitude: W122.35709
Road #: Mountain Highway #7
Nearest Town: Eatonville, WA
Access: Between Tacoma and Eatonville on Hwy #7 at mile post 35.3 there is an opening in the forest providing an unexpected but marvelous view east across a grass field to the mountain. On the left is some playground equipment belonging to the Tanwax Country Chapel, built in 2009, where there is ample parking in Chapel's parking lot. Immediately to the west is the Tanwax Greens Golf Course.

Rapjohn Lake

Latitude: N46.90554
Longitude: W122.34543
Road #: Mountain Highway #7
Nearest Town: Eatonville, WA
Access: Take Hwy #7 mile post 34, turn east on 384[th Ave.] S for 0.3 mile, then south on 62 Ave. S for 0.3 mile, or follow the sign to the public fishing area. Any place near the boat ramp or the hill leading to the ramp is a good to set up your tripod. Since this photo was taken, a cell tower was constructed where the tree line meets the mountain that creates an extra challenge to avoid seeing its flashing red beacon. The lake is 55 acres in size with a maximum depth of 18 feet.

Stringtown

Latitude: N46.887707
Longitude: W122.322517
Road #: Stringtown Road
Nearest Town: Eatonville, WA
Access: From the Mountain Highway #7 at mile post 34.9, turn east on the Stringtown Road for 1.9 miles. Note the "lenticular" cloud formation for which Mt. Rainier is famous since it can create its own weather pattern. Lenticular clouds (Altocumulus lenticularis) are stationary lens-shaped clouds that form at high altitudes, normally aligned perpendicular to the wind direction.

Ohop Valley

Latitude: N 46.876040
Longitude: W122.344087
Road #: WA Highway #7 (also known as Mountain Highway E)
Nearest Town: Eatonville, WA
Access: West of Eatonville on Hwy #7 at the Ohop Grange the view to the east overlooks the Ohop Valley. Where the trees provide an opening, it is possible to get this view directly from Hwy # 7 at mile post 31.5. Upslope of the highway there are a few private homes at the south end of 66th Ave. E that may be contacted for permission to set up your tripod.

Kreger Lake

Latitude: N46.86745
Longitude: W122.40216
Road #: 416th St. E
Nearest Town: Eatonville, WA
Access: West of Eatonville on Hwy #7 at the Ohop Grange, turn west on 416th St. E which turns into 22nd Ave. E for 3.4 miles to the end of the road. Ample parking is available at the gate to a private housing development with a view directly east overlooking Kreger Lake. The lake is 42 acres in size with a maximum depth of 12 feet. This photo was made late in the day in October.

Kreger Ranch

Latitude: N46.87198
Longitude: W122,401837
Road #: 22 nd Ave E
Nearest Town: Eatonville, WA
Access: West of Eatonville on Hwy #7 at the Ohop Grange, turn west on 416th St. E (King Flander Road) which turns into 22nd Ave. E, go approximately 3 miles and look on your left for the gated entrance to the farm. If the gate is closed you might have to shoot through the grated gate. Be respectful of private property rights.

416 th Street SE, School Bus

Latitude: N46.878981
Longitude: W122.378923
Road #: 416 th Street SE
Nearest Town: Eatonville, WA
Access: West of Eatonville on Hwy #7 at the Ohop Grange, turn west on 416th St. E (King Flander Road) and go to the intersection with Dean Kreger Road East. Just 100 yards east of the intersection is your spot. The school bus goes by at 3:30pm. There is a wide spot across the road for parking in a driveway to a farm.

Alder Lake Cemetery

Latitude: N46.79108
Longitude: W122.28775
Road #: Cemetery Road E.
Nearest Town: Eatonville, WA
Access: From Eatonville take Hwy #7 towards Elbe and turn on to the Lillie Dale Road, go 0.6 mile and turn right on Cemetery Road E and continue for one mile until you reach the Alder Lake Cemetery. There is parking for at least 13 vehicles. Walk to the water's edge and search for a vantage point viewing east. The first dam on the Nisqually River creating Alder Lake occurred in 1910 and a second dam was built in 1944, both by the Tacoma Public Utilities. These stumps, visible at lower water, are vivid reminders of the forest that was inundated.

Park Junction

Latitude: N46.75632
Longitude: W122.13312
Road #: Hwy #706
Nearest Town: Ashford, WA
Access: Between Elbe and Ashford at mile post 2.4 the old Ceccanti Ranch (no longer present) stood for many years providing some great photo opportunities to motorists on their way to Mt. Rainier National Park. The vantage point, however, is still excellent, especially if an elk herd wanders through this open field.

Gobbler's Knob

Latitude: N46.79269
Longitude: W121.96724
Road: Forest Road 59
Nearest Town: Ashford, WA
Access: From Huw #706 mile post 10.9 turn on to FR#59 for 7.1 miles, a windy gravel road suitable for most sedans, to the ridge top where the road turns sharply to the southwest. Parking is ample. There are views southeast to Gobbler's Knob, east to Mt. Rainier and north to Deer Cr., a tributary to the Puyallup River, and Glacier View Wilderness. This site and the one from Tipsoo Lake/Chinook Pass are the two having the closest locations to Mt. Rainier that are outside the park boundary and accessible by sedan. This site is 11 airline miles from the summit. Upon driving the 7.1 miles back to #706, take note of the Copper Creek Restaurant.

CHAPTER 2
VIEWING NORTH/NORTHEAST

Views of Mt. Rainier from the south looking north are almost as limited as from the north side looking south. My favorites are:

Skate Creek Road
Hugo Lake
Mineral Lake
Mineral

Skate Creek Road

Latitude: N46.72893
Longitude: W121.86523
Road #: Kernahan Road or FR #52
Nearest Town: Ashford, WA
Access: Between Elbe and Ashford on Hwy. #706 take Skate Creek Road, (aka Kernahan Road or FR #52) to mile post 7.6. The view is to the north and overlooks the Nisqually River. This road is closed in the winter.

Hugo Lake

Latitude: N46.45634
Longitude: W121.55243
Road #: FR #21
Nearest Town: Packwood, WA
Access: Take US #12 for 3.0 miles south of Packwood to mile post 128.6, turn on to FR #21 for 13.4 miles on a gravel road. Hugo Lake is 1.5 acres in size. Since this road is one of two routes to Walput Lake, it gets a great deal of use and can be a bumpy ride late in the year. Regardless, it's suitable for a sedan.

Mineral Lake

Latitude: N46.72330
Longitude: W122.18174
Road #: Mineral Hill Road7
Nearest Town: Mineral, WA
Access: From Hwy #7 take any of the three roads leading to downtown Mineral. Take the Mineral Road Hill Road north along the west side of Mineral Lake and look to the east. Seek permission from the land owner at the Mineral Lake Lodge.

Mineral

Latitude: N46.712441
Longitude: W122.209360
Road #: Mountain Hwy #7
Nearest Town: Mineral, WA
Access: Between Elbe and Morton on Hwy #7 at mile post 12.8 at the intersection with FR 74 the view is to the east across a field that has not changed since I first photographed this site in the fall of 1971. Parking is available on both sides of Hwy #7.

CHAPTER 3
VIEWING WEST

From the east side there are four sites accessible via Highway #410 and US #12 looking west.

Crystal Mountain (Summit House)
White River
Tipsoo Lake
White Pass

Crystal Mountain (Summit House)

Latitude: N46.935275
Longitude: W121.500343
Road #: Hwy #410
Nearest Town: Enumclaw, WA
Access: From Greenwater drive south on Hwy #410 towards the Mount Rainier National Park, turn left (north) on to the Crystal Mt. Ski area road, go to the end of the road which is the parking lot to ski area and take the gondola to the Summit House Restaurant which is 6,400 feet above sea level. This is one of the most spectacular views of Mt. Rainier and is most enjoyable while dinning in the restaurant or sitting outside. Although this view is available from inside the restaurant it is slightly better from outside restaurant. In the summer folding chairs and picnic tables dot the area in front of the restaurant providing for a near European Alps experience.

White River/410

Latitude: N46.900888
Longitude: W 121.543576
Road #: Hwy #410
Nearest Town: Enumclaw, WA
Access: From Enumclaw take Hwy #410 south to the area between mile posts 62.5 and 63.5. Parking is available on the gravel shoulder but since it is on the outside lane of the #410, great care is necessary when both parking and setting up your tripod.

Tipsoo Lake

Latitude: N46.869843
Longitude: W121.514792
Road #: Hwy #410
Nearest Town: Packwood, WA
Access: Take #123 or #410 to Chinook Pass and drive approximately 0.2 mile west on #410 and park on the right-hand side of the road in the designated WA Department of Transportation (DOT) parking area and walk east uphill to the end of the sidewalk where there is a wide spot perfect for setting up your tripod. The lake is at an elevation of 5,314 feet, 6.5 acres in size with a maximum depth of 15 feet. This road is closed in the winter.

White Pass

Latitude: N46.631978
Longitude: W121.448131
Road #: US #12
Nearest Town: Packwood, WA
Access: From Packwood drive 16.2 miles east on Highway #12 towards White Pass to MP 147.8. There is a newly constructed Mt. Rainier Viewpoint with plenty of room to park the largest of vehicles. Elevation of 3,822 feet.

CHAPTER 4
VIEWING SOUTH

Views from the highways and roads on the north side of Mt. Rainier are more limited than the west side. There is one major viewpoint at mile post 49 on Hwy. #410 called the Mather Parkway Viewpoint. It is maintained by the WA Department of Transportation but the view is limited to a narrow alley cut through the young forest.

Better views are available on the road to the Carbon River entrance to the park and from in and around the town of Orting.

Suntop Lookout
Carbon River
Orting
Enumclaw
Lake Tapps

Suntop Fire Lookout

Latitude: N47.041001
Longitude: W121.596524
Road #: Hwy #410
Nearest Town: Enumclaw, WA
Access: From Enumclaw take Hwy #410 to mile post 49.3, then right on FS 7300 and go 1.3 miles passing over the White River, turn left on FS 7315 for 4.9 miles to the top of a small pass, take a sharp right turn and head uphill pass the gate to the lookout elevation 5,280 feet. This U.S. Forest Service lookout is open from mid-June to the first snow fall.

Carbon River

Latitude: N47.01977
Longitude: W122.03913
Road #: Hwy #165S
Nearest Town: Wilkeson, WA
Access: From downtown Wilkeson, take Hwy #165 South for 5.8 miles where it intersects with the road to the Carbon River park entrance and Mowich Lake. Continue on Hwy #165 South for one mile to mile post 10.2. Parking is limited to the side of the road. The view is to the southeast across the Carbon River Valley. Continuing on this road will take you to Mowich Lake.

Orting

Latitude: N47.08886
Longitude: W122.21367
Road #: Orting-Kapowsin Highway East
Nearest Town: Orting, WA
Access: From downtown Orting at the intersection of Hwy #162 (Washington Ave. North) and the Orting-Kapowsin Highway East (Calistoga St. NW), go south on the Orting-Kapowsin Highway East for 0.7 mile to the bridge over the Puyallup River. Park at the south end of the bridge at the intersection of the Orting-Kapowsin Highway East and Leach Road East.

Enumclaw

Latitude: N47.199246
Longitude: W121.971298
Road #: Hwy #410
Nearest Town: Enumclaw, WA
Access: From downtown Enumclaw take Hwy #410 east approximately 0.5 mile for a view to the southeast overlooking this dairy farm. Today part of the farm has been replaced by a housing development.

Lake Tapps

Latitude: N47.239144
Longitude: W122.167795
Road #: Hwy #410
Nearest Town: Sumner, WA
Access: From Sumner near the intersection of Hwy #410 and Sumner Tapps Hwy. E. drive north on Sumner Tapps Hwy. E., turn right (east) on 16th St. Ct. E. which turns north and becomes 182nd, Ave. E., (passing the sign that says "Tacoma Point") and then turn right (east) on 9th St. E. which turns in 12 St. E. Watch for the sign "Lake Tapps County Park" and then right (south) on 198th Av. E. for one block which will take you into the park. A largely undeveloped 135-acre site with approximately 10,000 feet of waterfront access including a sandy swimming area. Open 6am to 8pm from April through September, 7:30am to 4pm from October through March.

CHAPTER 5
INSIDE THE PARK

Mount Rainier National Park is open all year but as of May 24, 2024 there is a reservation system from 7am to 3pm. Visitation is at its peak in July and August, when the weather is warm and dry and the wildflowers are blooming. Parking is limited in many areas of the park especially on busy summer weekends and holidays. If you are planning a summer trip to Mount Rainier, consider visiting mid-week, which is generally less crowded. In spring, with ephemeral waterfalls and in autumn, with brilliant colors reaching deep into the valleys, visitors can enjoy a more leisurely vacation in the park. During these seasons, weather may determine the availability of facilities in certain areas of the park. Before making any plans check the current status of roads, campgrounds, trails and activities. Inside the park the number of locations from which to photograph Mt. Rainier are numerous, however, I have listed some of the most common that have convenient and safe parking. These locations are displayed in a counterclockwise direction around the mountain.

Vehicle access to Mount Rainier National Park in the winter is only available from the Nisqually Entrance, in the southwest corner of the park on the way to Paradise. The Carbon River Entrance is open but the road within the park boundary is limited to foot and bicycle traffic. Check the road status prior to coming to the park as road conditions are subject to change.

Some of the best views of Mt. Rainier are from the highway traversing Mount Rainier National Park. There are four major entrances to the park.

Nisqually: This point of entry is on the southwest corner of the park on Hwy #706 coming from Ashford. This is the primary route to Longmire and Paradise.

Ohanapecosh: This point of entry is on the southeast corner of the park on Hwy #123 coming from Packwood.

Sunrise (White River): This point of entry is on the east side of the park on Hwy #410 coming from Enumclaw and also from Yakima via Chinook Pass.

Carbon River: This point of entry is on the northwest corner of the park on Hwy #165 coming from Wilkeson. Vehicle travel beyond the entrance is not possible due to repeat flooding that destroyed the road and bridges.

Kautz Creek

Latitude: N46.736410
Longitude: W121.856950
Road #: Hwy #706 (Paradise Road East) within the Mt. Rainier National Park
Nearest Town: Ashford, WA
Access: Within the Mount Rainier National Park between the Nisqually Entrance and Longmire, Kautz Creek intersects the Paradise Road. The Kautz Creek drainage, tributary to the Nisqually River, has been ravaged by floods (1947), decimated by fires, and rearranged by mud slides. Floods in November 2006 created a new channel for the creek that now crosses the highway a short distance to the east of where this photo was taken.

Ricksecker Point

Latitude: N46.770602
Longitude: W121.780479
Road #: Hwy #706 (Paradise Road East) within the Mt. Rainier National Park
Nearest Town: Ashford, WA
Access: Within the Mount Rainier National Park between Longmire and Paradise take the road across the Nisqually River and then take the loop road to Ricksecker Point. Although this loop road is closed in the winter it is accessible all other times of the year and parking is plentiful. If you encounter snow, this site is a short walk from the main road.

Unnamed Pull Out

Latitude: N46.77763
Longitude: W121.76167
Road #: Hwy #706 (Paradise Road East) within the Mt. Rainier National Park Nearest Town:
Nearest Town: Ashford, WA
Access: Within the Mount Rainier National Park between Longmire and Paradise take the Paradise Valley Road across the Nisqually River and past Ricksecker Point. This unnamed pullout will be on your left. This photo was taken from the driver's seat.

Paradise Visitor Center

Latitude: N46.785594
Longitude: W121.73609
Road #: Hwy #706 (Paradise Road East) within the Mt. Rainier National Park
Nearest Town: Ashford, WA
Access: Within the Mount Rainier National Park, take the Paradise Road to the Paradise Visitor Center. The new Henry M. Jackson Memorial Visitor Center was completed in 2008. The Center is a day-use facility located in the Paradise area. This facility offers exhibits, films, guided ranger programs, a book store, a snack bar, and a gift shop, as well as public restrooms, and informational brochures and maps. This photo was made in early October.

Paradise Creek

Latitude: N46.78220
Longitude: W121.72801
Road #: Hwy #706 (Paradise Road East) within the Mt. Rainier National Park
Nearest Town: Ashford, WA
Access: Within the Mount Rainier National Park, from the Paradise Visitor Center exit the parking lot heading downhill on the one-way Paradise Creek Road and look for a view back to the mountain. Paradise Lodge is visible on the left side of the photo at the mid-point. This photo was taken while cross country skiing. Although this road is closed in the winter the view is accessible all other times of year and is especially colorful in the fall.

Reflection Lake (west)

Latitude: N46.76898
Longitude: W121.73252
Road #: Hwy #706 (Paradise Road East) within the Mt. Rainier National Park
Nearest Town: Ashford, WA
Access: From the Nisqually entrance at the southwest corner of the park, take the main highway towards Paradise and turn right on the Stevens Canyon Road heading towards Yakima. Go approximately 1.5 miles to the public parking area overlooking this 13-acre subalpine lake. This site is located at the west end of the parking lot. There is a trail that provides access along the shoreline. Watch for signs limiting access to the actual shoreline because it is an environmentally sensitive area.

Reflection Lake (east)

Latitude: N46.769242
Longitude: W121.72459
Road #: Hwy #706 (Paradise Road East) within the Mt. Rainier National Park
Nearest Town: Ashford, WA
Access: Both the west and east lakes provide some of the best vantage points from which to photograph Mt. Rainier and they are located within the Mt. Rainier National Park. Parking for the east lake is limited but there is one place along the road to safely park. Use of a graduated filter can help balance the difference in lighting between the white snow-capped mountain and the darker water. This photo was made in early October, mid-afternoon, just after the mountain ash and huckleberry plants had turned color.

Stevens Canyon

Latitude: N46.763960
Longitude: W121.695790
Road #: Hwy #706 (Stevens Canyon Road) within the Mount Rainier National Park
Nearest Town: Packwood, WA
Access: Within the Mount Rainier National Park, just east of Reflection Lakes and northeast of Bench Lake the road makes a very sharp hairpin turn that provides a spectacular view of Stevens Canyon and Mt. Rainier. There is ample parking on the shoulder of the road.

Backbone Ridge

Latitude: N46.710951
Longitude: W121.600793
Road #: Hwy #706 (Stevens Canyon Road) within the Mount Rainier National Park
Nearest Town: Packwood, WA
Access: Within the Mount Rainier National Park, between Paradise and the Stevens Canyon entrance off Hwy #123, Backbone Ridge vista is a large pullout that is one of few in the park suitable for large or long vehicles. In recent years the trees have grown tall enough to block part of this great view.

Box Canyon

Latitude: N46.766364
Longitude: W121.635714
Road #: Hwy #706 (Stevens Canyon Road) within the Mount Rainier National Park
Nearest Town: Packwood, WA
Access: Within the Mount Rainier National Park, between Paradise and the Stevens Canyon entrance off Hwy #123, Box Canyon is a wide U-shaped valley carved by the Cowlitz Glacier whose terminus is three miles upstream. Glacial striations carved by the rasping action of rocks frozen into the glacier's bed can be seen on the smooth, rounded bedrock outcrops on the right. Both highway and foot bridge span the Muddy Fork Cowlitz River. Ample parking is available just past the tunnel and bridge as well as rest rooms.

Sunrise Point Lookout

Latitude: N46.769242
Longitude: W121.723732
Road#: Sunrise Road within the Mt. Rainier National Park
Nearest Town: Enumclaw, WA
Access: From Hwy #410 take the White River entrance (Mather Memorial Parkway) heading southwest for approximately 50 miles. Sunrise Point Lookout is a parking area on a hairpin turn. The view is west to the mountain.

Sunrise Visitor's Center

Latitude: N46.913768
Longitude: W 121.631039
Road #: Sunrise Road within the Mt. Rainier National Park
Nearest Town: Enumclaw, WA
Access: From Hwy #410 take the White River entrance (Mather Memorial Parkway) heading southwest. The road ends at the Sunrise Visitor Center. At 6,400 feet above sea level, Sunrise is the highest point in the park that you can reach by vehicle and is open from July to late September. The meadows abound with wildflowers. On clear days Sunrise provides breathtaking views of Mt. Rainier, Emmons Glacier, and many other volcanoes in the Cascade Range.

I am closing this first volume of the **PHOTOGRAPHER'S GUIDE TO WASHINGTON'S BEST VIEWS** with a view of the summit taken during that brief period late in the day when the last rays of sunlight graze the highest snow-covered parts of our amazing planet creating that magic Alpenglow. I hope you find this book fun and helpful as you search for the perfect photograph. Enjoy.

THE SUMMIT OF MT. RAINIER
Lat: N46.85289
Long: W121.76037
Elevation: 14,410 feet

www.ingramcontent.com/pod-product-compliance
Lightning Source LLC
Chambersburg PA
CBHW041551120626
46551CB00002B/169